WALK WITH ME

A Poetry and Prose Collection

by

Fatima Siraj

www.fatimasiraj.com

ISBN 978-969-23231-0-9

Attention schools and businesses: Walk with Me is
available at quantity discounts with bulk purchase
for educational, business or sales promotional use.
For information, please email: sales@fatimasiraj.com

FIRST EDITION

For my dad,
thank you for your unconditional support.

Foreword

I am slowly starting to learn about the things that our parents hid from us when we were young - that getting lost in the middle of the street is not an adventure, that losing things does not lead us to unravelling mysteries and that a hostel room doesn't just evoke a sense of freedom but the smell of old laundry resting in the corner of the room.

While the anxiety of being "well settled" echoes in my head, I must be mindful of over sharing during long conversations with friends and maintain a safe distance so I don't overstep the un-defined boundaries of "privacy".

In 2017, I can step outside the traditional gender role - but in 2017, I am struggling with a personal identity crisis while discovering the society's description of an ideal relationship. I must check in on a full stomach at a fine dining restaurant - add my location and move on, because in 2017, we are all scrambling for a view from a New York City apartment and we all have a separate definition for 'struggle'.

18

I'm afraid of turning 18.
As if after this time everything will seem to have aged
a little. Beauty of this sentiment is that it allows me
to dream; but the struggle is to hold on. As if I'll no
longer be capable of falling head over heels for the
boy who smiles across the room from me, or believe
that I'll have enough money to travel the world.
Being 18 seems daunting. Everyone will think I'm an
adult when the truth is I'll be just as confused as I
am right now. Does turning 18 mean I'll get over the
heartache of 16, because when I'm 19 I'm sure it
won't matter. I'm scared of stepping into the realities
of 18. True love won't bring you flowers everyday but
they may show it by just being there – will my 18-
year-old-self think that's romantic? I won't be able to
make a list of all the things I want because slowly
it'll become the exact moment for which I was
planning. What will I do when they tell me to become
independent, and what will I do when I'm not in that
university or in that job or in that house; will my
younger self be proud of being optimistic or
pronounce these dreams as a pile of regrets? I don't
know if turning 18 will make it all better but I'll get
to blow a candle, to make a wish, that as I grow
older I am only content with the decisions I have
made.

THERE ARE TWO WORLDS

(one i was born in, the second my father gave)

The world as you know it –

Is an egg-shaped phenomenon rotating about its axis that bulges from the equator and is flattened at the poles.

Do you know what happened?

When I was born, my father took this world and molded it into a sphere. Like a perfectly rolled clay ball, he dried it under the shade – for the sun would have given it cracks. He outlined and labelled each continent – places he thought I would admire in my photography and poetry and paintings. He colored it blue and green so that it may soothe my eyes. In the end, when he was satisfied that he had put all his effort and everything more, he lay this tiny sphere of clay onto my palms.

He didn't tell me that it was fragile, to ensure I wouldn't be disappointed when people fell off their pedestals. He didn't size it to fit the measurements of my palms, to provide me with the ability to look beyond my own existence. He didn't say that it was only mine – because he wanted to share it with me.

The world as I know it –

Had never been flawed to begin with.

AN ADVENTURE

He runs –
room to room
dirties his hands with
dust bunnies under the bed
and scrapes his knees
from jumping onto chairs
higher than his height
and when he finds
a string of woolen thread
near the corner
where the cupboard stands

he sits –
to wrap it around his hand
unwraps it on the other hand
he holds it between his toes
eventually understanding
that it's used to tie a knot
so, he looks down intently
attempting to make a loop
which is never the right size

when the fascination of
strings and knots runs dry

off to another room –
you'll find him sitting in another corner
with all the same excitement
because a child thinks
all is worthy
until tucked in bed safely
with a promise, of
a new adventure tomorrow.

FIRST DAY OF SCHOOL

She promised she'd sit outside my classroom
until the school bell rang good-bye
but the windows had been covered by posters of
animals
and i couldn't see my mother
so i cried, unafraid of who saw my cheeks blush
until the teacher called my mother
and let me go back home,
on the first day of school.

Today, i walk through another door
an establishment, i've been told
will transform my life
by providing a new perspective –
but how could i have learned to observe
when windows had always been hidden
and i'd been taught to stare at walls.

They won't understand how
a place can hold back my learning
because i don't feel i belong here
i will always be a misfit
with a heart put at compromise
this time i can only cry on the inside.

Find me another place,
i don't belong here.

MIND VS HEART

I have restricted my mind to serve as a moral compass.

I wouldn't know of a reply that is
proper and timely and clear

you'll hear gasps of astonishment
in the transition from small talk to gossip.

I wouldn't know when to lower my voice
or how to queue sentences
according to time.

Sometimes I'll smile before I speak.

If my face is only a dull scenery
you'll understand my heart was never invested.

BEYOND REPAIR

We're all a little malfunctioned
but with a different screw unhinged

i'll tell you of the defects
i've self-created
if you reveal the faults
you've carried from birth.

SHELL

Tonight
i make a prayer,

god, reveal my flaws

so i may learn
to better hide them

behind the fabric of my skin
i claim to resemble a *shell.*

A HANGER

I am a hanger in his closet
he keeps as a back up
when he runs out of pockets
i am there to clean up.

DEAR DOCTOR

The universe ~~is~~ appears
stronger in my mind
folded in sleeps
cloaked in dreams

in a different realm
i do not scream
i am not suffering
from a broken dream.

A DISCOVERY

There are abandoned buildings

inside of me.

NOT ENOUGH

I have met people
who made the universe
sound incompetent.

As if the galaxies
do not have the strength
to carry a human being
like me.

ERROR

We do not speak the same language
i say 'i miss you'
(i'm longing you)
i say 'i need you'
(i'm craving you)

to him,
        they define distance
for me,
        they're gaps in our survival.

PERMISSION

Sit him down
ask him "what are the three things my daughter
likes?"
Do not be proud
when your daughter's answer resembles his's

but say yes
when he mentions a trait
you realize,
could only be observed through his eyes.

EPIPHANY

"gosh! it's like you're in here..."
"what do you mean?" i asked.

"it's like i can't get rid of you or
that thing which i don't remember
and it's bothering me why i cannot
recall my dinner from last night
because i am sure i had gone to bed
thanking God for how happy i was"

the vein within my right leg
is threatening to implode
from the anxiety accumulating
and resisting to let go

"can you stop?" it says

i just want to breathe –
the morning is still and cool
and a little peaceful,
despite the car engines
i can hear across the road

"what do you mean?"

and wasn't it me complaining
how it had come into my head
and stolen the place within
which was meant to be resetting goals
and my body, it was supposed to cook me
an omelet, because i haven't had it for days
so i ask again, louder this time
"what do you mean?"
"no one is here, but you."

*[the living room floor board creaks as I split the
egg in two]*

HIS SCENT

I felt music in my ears and the ground began to slip,
I had lost control. It was the good kind - where you
want to remain dizzy, to feel there is something
within you which had been rigid but a power greater
than existence is eclipsing you within its reach.

I wanted to remain there - within your touch, the
sound of your rhythmic heartbeat echoed in my ears.
It swung my senses like a pendulum.

To and fro.

My neck craned to consider your foggy eyes, the
smoke engulfed me. The smoke curled into the fabric
of my skin. I held onto you - i was about to fall.
When you decided to step closer and whisper mint-
like syllables, tasting like saffron and honey - they
circled my tongue like a foreigner admiring silk for
the first time. I felt myself lean against your chest,
and i fell into a trance i haven't been able to recover
from since.

DON'T DO THIS

Don't do this –
i know it's not my place,
i promise never to interfere again.

Don't put yourself to sleep –
with colored pills, none of us have seen before
you say it's insomnia,
but please try singing the lullaby,
you tell me, will sing to your child one day.

Don't close the door on me –
you probably think i'm ranting,
trying to fit my story into yours,
but it's only to encourage you
to tell me more, about how your day had been.

Don't say you hate me –
the lights need not be turned off
adjusting itself to melancholic music,
you had shunned off at the record store,
just the day before.

Don't do this –
i know it's not my place,
i promise never to interfere again.

ANXIETY leads to
unfulfilled obligations,
unattended parties,
unfinished projects

constant doubt
careless conversations
conditional confrontations

anxiety is not a choice
it leads to self-deprecation.

MEMOIR

Maybe the only way to forget you
is by writing my memoir,
at least then
my writings won't have to be about you
but i'll probably end up telling
how i came about myself,
in meeting you.

HOW DOES DESTINY WORK?

Right now –
we are accumulating a series of mistakes.

Later –
we will label it as time.

Distinguishing them as the good times
and the bad times –
the bad times are better to remain in the past.

Tomorrow –
supposedly glorious
reputably untouched
destiny will define tomorrow.

But how does destiny work?

The mistakes happened
the way they did
as they were meant to
but if i hadn't made the mistake,
things would have been different?

∞

It was the way you called me mortal,
that made me believe in infinity otherwise.

HOW DO YOU REMEMBER ME?

Every toss and turn on a sleepless night,
i'm struck with a tingling feeling
that includes a thought of you.

I've been trying to forget
the way you smiled at me,
there were too many people in the room that day
so you had to look away.

My throat gets a little dry
when i trace back to the days
you'd message me at 4 am
asking if i was still awake,
your sleepy voice would ask me to stay
because you thought talking to me made your day.

I can't erase that you mentioned,
you wished we had met earlier
so you could have told me more of your childhood
stories.

I've chosen to remember
the way you made me feel special.

It makes more sense this way.

WE DIDN'T WANT THIS

Most of don't figure out
until present seems to have elapsed
we joke about the nonsensical events,
proclaiming them as the foolish mistakes we already
made
while we cough up on the cigarette smoke
a tear falls
when we think about an old friend
who chose to leave us,
as we stare at an old photograph –
torn in half, decorated in a rusty frame
what happens to the dust we've collected in our
drawers?
hoping for it to be carried away by air
while we keep our windows closed

Will we ever call our parents?

Confessing that we let our prejudice get the best of
us
or will we send a holiday card,
once again,
announcing,
"we are happier than the year before."

Our neighbor may have called us
to babysit their children for a night
but
we let it to go to voicemail as we eat our takeaway
pasta,
convincing us that it tastes the same –
like it used to
at the weekends spent at our grandparents' house.

If we hear a knock on the door,
will we rush to open?
eager to see a friendly face,

who knows –
maybe it's the same opportunity we answered to
years ago
and look where it got us now.

So we put our blinders down,
Praying,
that somebody will return soon.

SHAPES

I've been losing control
like a child struggling to color within the lines
without understanding the contours,
of a shape he is un-known to
but observing only after,
if it resembles the one he had been promised.

I stare at the dark night, dotted with stars
trying to remember the constellations
i've only ever seen in the books
"perhaps creating my own would be better":
i think to myself.

After all, it's just one star to another
closer to where i started,
i'm chasing after a shape
bound to remain incomplete.

CORSAGE

And i know that we will both be there
he is going to be holding a corsage for her
and he will put on his fancy suit
with the tie of the color i like

he will look at me
but –
he won't smile
because we stopped sharing that act of lie
a long time back

he'll walk past me,
softer and swifter than the wind
he'll go up to her and laugh

he'll pretend to be having the time of his life
because he knows that'd hurt me
when i turn around,
he'll look at me but never say,
wondering where we had gone wrong
and i'll cry
that day,
i'll know that we had shared a night.

RESERVED

Our tears and emotions have been duly reserved for the ones who have left us along the way – especially the ones who carry roses and abuse the words *forever* and *love*. But there are also those taking vows, making promises, throwing compliments and letting them evaporate as soon as they meet the atmosphere. what about those who crossed their hearts and announced to be present in our hardest times with certainty or those who took the responsibility of bringing us bad news and letting us cry on their shoulders? Often, we've forgotten the people who kindly whispered *no* when we asked for their help –

At least it was their honesty that broke our hearts.

STRESS

It creeps up on you
s l o w l y
and then all at once –

Difficult to realize the
implications of this sentiment
until the doctor asks:
"have you been stressed?"
and you worry, if the cracks in your voice
resonate the thumping in your chest

like a bullet through a window,
serving shattered glass as a reminder –
that all the air had been locked out
of the headspace, you had reserved for something
else
will you clasp your chest tightly
with a palm to spread the warmth

and let the tears ooze out
s l o w l y
and then all at once?

OUR UNIVERSE

When we opened our eyes for the first time in this world, they pronounced us *innocent*. We carried a presence that brought joy to those who knew us and a hope for those who wanted to believe that the world, unlike they knew of, is pure.

As we grew older, the stark vividness of reality started to consume us. Each day became a task and the people a mere formality. Some people became an asset to help us achieve that task and others an obstacle. Why we thought this way? Because reality was told to be beyond our control and each one believed they could defy the shackles of universe, holding each atom in its place. We were told that stars couldn't merge into the oceans and birds flew higher than our heads could tilt, that the strength of the sun's rays was something to stay protected from. For those who were told of a divine, godly presence - started to believe in miracles. That something beyond our control may well be within our reach. So we poured our hearts out, hoping that an omnipotent being is catching our tears. We left it up to nature and miracles and luck. Too bad, we weren't conscious enough to look for signs within our imperfect reality and we let our hopes fall to ground.

If only we knew that the world wasn't acting against us - we'd take a moment to occupy responsibility in the place where our hearts have become hollow. Realize that each decision is within our spread and the actions we take need not be perfect, unlike the cosmos holding us together.

I suppose when we opened our eyes, they should have told us we'd spend our whole lives hanging onto a tarnish of hope.

SOUVENIR

Travelling is meant to teach us to move on,
however, as the number of souvenirs i collect
mount on my bookshelf,

the memories leave a void

of its intimacy.

MONUMENT

i
am a
monument
of regrets and resentments,
they worship me for happiness.

BARE SOIL

You say, there is no way out –

But aren't you standing on bare soil,
which is begging for pavements and directions?

BEARINGS

I used to think that you couldn't ever know someone
after holding a string of the same dreams
i thought that when two souls collided
they'd have enough power to re-define themselves
after an impact
but without creating insurmountable distances
i wondered how it would feel
when a gush of wind holding memories would swish
by,
messing my bearings-
i'd look around to see if the person was still next to
me
assured that nothing has changed yet
although i'm facing north,
at the exact spot, you left me at
the rope knotted,
you're not here.

POSSIBILITIES

I supposed we made our own possibilities
if the distance far, we'd make the timing work
if the time scarce, we'd postpone all that mattered
less
if it mattered, we'd give it a chance –
wait a little longer,
smile a bit more,
watch our step?
but lately,
everything seems out of control
taking out the batteries doesn't stop time anymore
when you said,

"miracles can happen sometimes, you know",

i realized we were trying to fight something bigger
than the both of us,
as if we knew how impossible we were
that we would require magic to make it work
almost as if that magic didn't exist –
like we weren't supposed to exist together

after all,
we shouldn't need a miracle to prove our love.

TOYS

I belong from a generation which had the privilege of each having their own Mr. Teddy. I remember I would snuggle its fluffy chest and let it sleep beside me. The next morning, I would wake up to see that while it laid upside down, its smile had remained the same. My siblings and I learnt how to compete with zeal by attempting to build the tallest structure out of blocks that was possible. And when the buildings collapsed into a rubble, we gave flight to paper planes that never made it far enough.

With age, creativity began aligning itself with logic, - our tiny hands would stare at pieces of cardboard puzzles, attempting to match it with the picture illustrated on the box. Once a puzzle was solved in place, we'd never look back at it again. Soon, scratching stickers off our bicycles became an adventurous hobby and when we learned to paddle its wheel, it started to seem as if we had never had to learn how to walk.

We transitioned from stuffed toys to wheels on the street. This transformation was marked through the complexity of toys that emerged from our birthday gifts. Gleaming with excitement, we'd forget to eat our birthday cakes and the decorations seemed as if they were only there for the sake of it.

Today we lean back on our stuffed toys which provide our backs the support they require, we realize that the bright screens will never be enough to replicate the emotional transformation that these toys had granted us.

UNTIL THEN

"i wish i had met someone like you before"

believe me, he meant it

not in that unmeasurable moment
or with a cup of gin in his hands
or on those magical nights that hypnotize you to
confess

he meant it
in the purest of his thoughts

he loved the way your long hair followed a breeze,
he adored it when you confused names when telling
a story
how you made up words just to describe him
he'd watch you collect flowers and yearn to be one of
them-
the delicate petals you collected
and threw them on his hair
he never minded that they clustered his hair
your fragrance is still engulfed in his senses
for he searches for it still
he looks at your polaroid
hoping,
that someone would resemble it
he loved you in every way possible –

but remember,
he wished to find "someone like you"
and until he has,
he will always remember you

until.

then.

NO GOODBYE

From the places i've been to –
i recall the people i've missed or those who let go
over time
those who grew apart or those who chose to keep
distance
i remember of the first time that they said hello
but can never chase down the goodbye
that should have come with their absence
the smile which made me believe they were kind,
or the embrace that showed me warmth
or the touch that made me feel at ease
how is it that those who've left have had the greatest
impact only after?
only after the unsaid promise of 'staying in touch',
the half-murmured whisper of 'i'll miss you',
un-granted wish of 'i won't forget you, we'll meet
again'
and where was the tear that came with 'i must leave
now',
with a half empty thought- alas!
i realize that their absence was the goodbye.

AN ARTIST'S DILEMMA

I swear,
we are not the "perfectionists"
we call ourselves

We're scared of getting it wrong
so, we trace our steps
until they lose their shape
and we have to start
all over again.

AM I STILL THERE?

When i turned around
and the shadow left
steps slowly distanced
and i faded into the horizon
did you wonder why i could not be seen
or why i had walked away
perhaps not the why
at least you must have noticed that i was gone
did it feel like everything had changed?

I AM A ROBOT

"Don't you know that you were supposed to wake up? Look at the time! You're late (again). What are the paintbrushes doing on the carpet? The stains won't ever leave. I do not know when you will come to realize that you are wasting your time. This is not why we provide for you – how is it so easy for you to step outside of the box and believe that what you're doing is worthwhile?

Come on, wake up already! You've got to eat breakfast, hold your briefcase and sit in front of the computer screen from nine to five because that will make us proud. Your sitting idle on a top floor of a glass building which can only look out will be the symbol of success."

The words vibrate the upper cortex of my brain; I am unable to comprehend the sheets of data lying in front of me. A couple of robots reminded me that I should have deciphered the code by now. They left another pile of files and papers with an unknown language. I notice that I had been taught to write and speak these unfamiliar words because they said it'd help me when I got out into the world. I am trying to remember their meaning. I am a stranger to them and the words are starting to hurt.

I have a migraine. I think I should go home. I read the clock. It says 1 pm. Lunchtime, I remember. Automatically, I pick up my phone and rush down to the hawker outside the building. I buy a bagel. I hear people whispering around me, reminding themselves that it's too expensive to afford a decent lunch. But this is not why I bought a bagel. I like the crumbs that fall with each bite, reminding me that existence is composed of tiny bits.

My body drags itself near the elevator. My finger
presses the button for the twentieth floor. I look
around, there are robots in uniform. They only smile
before entering the elevator, a few of the trained
robots also say goodbye. Their automation left them
blank in between the two greetings; therefore, they
cannot formulate conversations. As light above the
elevator door blinks for TWENTY, I realize that my
body had not transmitted neurons before alerting my
finger to press for this specific level of the building.

The migraine has ended, there is an itch in my legs. I
can't stop them from shaking. I open the inescapable
bright screen. Someone has sent me an email. The
itch has stopped. I am staring at the same language
again. It is bigger this time, the words are shouting
at me. I breathe. I try to calm down. I look outside
the window.
The cars swish past and robots are walking without
making an eye contact. They seem to know what
they're doing. I knock on the window, to talk to those
robots. Ask them where they were made. I knock
harder – the window doesn't break. My knocks do
not create a noise.
I am trapped.

(My algorithm had been fixed before I came here.)

LET'S CATCH UP!

"hello."
"hi, how've you been."
"i'm good, you?"
"same, it's been forever."
"yeah Imy we should meet up sometime."
"yes."
(seen)

The internet has become a wonderful way to soothe our conscious. The closeness of our friendship is indicated by the secret groups we make on WhatsApp and Instagram accounts which mention:"add up if we've talked at least once at 3am". We show off our bond by editing funny pictures and post it on Facebook and when a bunch of comments line up from the people we had intended it would reach, our conscious gains a sense of approval. What happened to ringing random neighbor's doorbell's and running away, showing up uninvited early in the morning or spending way too much time in the skatepark and secretly spray-painting walls we knew would look less ugly and more artistic. I'm not blaming the internet for taking up our lives – after all, we invite it ourselves. In quantities, we blame time for not being enough and power banks on low charging. Our relationships have become a profile picture and distances are marked by "Turn location on". Before we let our creativity dive into the unknown, we browse the Pinterest's boards of people we've never met. To see what is trending, to decide whether our ideas will be approved by avatars on the other side of the world. Soothe your conscious, my dear friend, but not through the illusions of photoshop. Get inspired – by the nature outside. I hope you learn to balance reality with a hint of glimmer that shines through the world that exists inside our screens.

PERFECT MATCH

It's so scary thinking
someday someone you know so well today
will only be a stranger
intimidating,
that you may never find someone like them;
if,
and when,
you do,
the resemblances are so starkly vivid
for a tiny minuscule second you forget every person
is unique
maybe this is what our purpose is,
know them,
love them,
leave them
although forgetting all would be so sensational;
but with every face in an unknown crowd you'd have
a memory to match
perhaps then you'll find your perfect match.

PERFECT MOMENT

It's unbelievable finding someone so similar to you
that you can almost feel your essence in them
it's rare; but the moment they touch your soul
through their words,
the way they smile- acknowledging you alone,
how the sound of your name
the most beautiful symphony sliding off their lips
that unique and unspoken feeling of
knowing that somewhere –
someone,
amidst a hundred people,
has a single thought of you?
that thought becomes almost within your reach
close enough to grasp
if you extend your arms at the exact moment
but that's the struggle, isn't it?
that perfect moment –
so invisible,
so absent.

FULFILLMENT

I paced back and forth in my bedroom,
while the squeaks of the wooden floor echoed
downstairs
i closed the door
only to notice
there weren't any sounds left to escape from
when i changed my phone
but realized a week after,
i hadn't told anyone of my new number,
or that the numbers on speed dial
carried names of people whose surnames i did not
know.
when i stared at the accolades hanging on my wall,

why is it that the only flashback
which occurred to me
was of my brother shouting my name from the
bleachers,
when they called my name for the graduating class?

sometimes i wonder,
with a hint of excitement i cannot relate to anymore,

weather the coffee shop my boyfriend used to drag
me to
still put extra whip cream on their black coffee,
that he used to hate so much

but it has been years
and i doubt he feels the same way

since i left in vain –
and forgot to pray for fulfillment.

END

Does it happen to you too?
that when he waves goodbye
and begins to leave,
you wish that he would turn around
part of you is almost certain that he will
although you know that he must leave
weather he looks back or not,
eventually there'd be an empty space next to yours,
from where he stood

but when he doesn't,
it almost feels as if your scent is beginning to fade off
his memory,
you just stand there; clenching onto his scarf –
making sure that you don't forget his
after all, goodbyes are not the end.

SEASONS

The plants grew years
and their hearts apart

on a road paved with stones
they watered gravel for flowers to grow.

SEA

You want to know why i'm quiet,
ask of my:
    1. fears
    2. dreams
    3. wishes
    4. hopes
    5. all the magic
i oh so wish it existed,
you ask me why i hide myself
from what everyone chases

it was magic i chased –

the prayer: in it i begged for you.

It fell, a drop-
i thought was rain
but with my tears you created a sea
deep enough for you to swim
and i to be drowned.

THE FIGHT

They had spent moments together
hand in hand,
never wanting to leave the room
but what trails back in their consciousness from the
first few days
is the squabble they had at his mother's house -
always needing to be at a side
for a refugee from the words
that cut through the promises made on long nights
he throws a glass,
rummaging through the drawers,
hoping to find something to hold onto
she screams
her voice screeching through the wall
in vain, she'd feel the warmth of his lips on hers
he takes a walk
tracing back to the same road
they had promised to walk together on
and when they meet at the same place she had
confessed 'i love you'
they realize
the fight only means
they're still willing to try.

THE HITCHHIKER

It was given we were destined to part ways at some
point
when the thought of us running into each other in a
new city started to feel too out of reach, i'd imagine
you thinking of me.

A sweet serenade –

And if i heard the mention of your name,
i'd go back to the day we met at a dinner
an allusion that it wasn't too long back
but i learnt too late
that when a road bends
and converges into a new street
it usually meets another place
i suppose the distance we covered together
wasn't long enough
for you to remember,
when our feet got tired
perhaps our mistake was to ask for help
and i suppose we never blamed
the hitchhiker,
who made us lose our way?

FREEDOM

To be able to say 'no'
to a boy on a drunken night
and to walk alone
without any place to be
to drive through the streets
with no vehicles in your way
being able to confess in churches
or to sit on its steps to cry
to dial a number
but letting it hang up
saying you need to talk,
but laughing at passerby's instead
to swim in waters
with the dress, you took on rent
waking up in the morning,
looking outside a new window sill again
to never having to return home
is this the freedom they beg for in their sleeps?

THE MISSING PIECE

Sometimes it all breaks down to the simplest of division. A second, a letter, a monomer; the unaccountable bits coming together as a whole. The broken pieces reminding you of the little things you have lost. So you just stare at them because trying to fix would only make the scars more visible. The small crack, a missing page, a forgotten memory – all that you've held onto for so long. You hold on tightly to the side of your bed, helping you to get up, readjusting to the surreal hollowness. Where are you? Who created these scars? Was it your own fault or of the person you've chosen to forget? Did you hurt anyone or were they making you say the words out loud? Was what you felt in that heartbeat of a moment your purest thought and was your decision to give up on the relationship you once took pride in, the humblest of your decision?Because when these simple pieces come together with your invisible movement of thoughts, they make a one. And that one is you. These little pieces' ensemble what you are today. Today is the put together puzzle of yesterday and i swear to god that's a puzzle. For if we could figure ourselves out, there would be nothing. You'd be one but with no simple re-defining pieces. So, you continue collecting these broken pieces, the acquaintances, and the commemorations. You let these be the unaccounted pieces so the puzzle doesn't finish and you keep creating a more wholesome you. You keep going for another second, another day, letting it come together because nothing feels better than the dream of a more perfect tomorrow and the satisfaction of blaming it on 'a missing piece'. You can't apologize and you can't cry. Fragile tears have no strength to compensate – for the pieces you have collected and the pieces you have lost along the way. All these pieces yearning they'll become a whole.

ADVICE FROM MY INSECURE SELF

Don't you tell me –
"i was thinking of you last night"
i'll only presume
you had put me off the whole day

if i don't believe you –
say, it was because
the night seemed longer than the day.

TEA

Sometimes when I sit down on a quiet evening, with a cup of warm tea held between my two hands and a book laid on my legs, a series of thoughts encompass my mind; resisting to let go. And I wonder if these are the thoughts that are holding me back from enjoying my tea.

Sometimes I forget to put sugar in it but the first sip still tastes the same. I suppose that's the mechanism of expectations. If you believe something for long enough, it becomes a part of you. Like the sweetness of sugar on my tongue encircling my mouth; yet the tea is bland.

As each thought occurs with an arithmetic sequence of sips, I remember that my mother had asked for some too but I only made for one and only the tea - leaves are remaining at the bottom of the cup.

FLAWS

i never knew what i wanted, so i was told to embrace
my strengths and turn it into fortunes. i didn't know
where i wanted to be but i was sure my strength laid
somewhere between long paragraphs carrying
unsolicited advice, but i grew rather skeptic about
the reliance of defeated warriors and imprisoned
princesses.

when the sound of uncertainty grew tiring to my
ears, i took to follow the advice of those who failed
before me and those who were doomed to after. until
i questioned whether my strength laid in the crisp
harshness of my weaknesses – the torn, untouched
parts that even myself hid from. the stories i didn't
tell, the people i didn't meet, the tasks i
procrastinated and the confrontations i avoided. the
places i ran away from, all because they carried a
specific memory. very soon, i learnt that it was the
ignorance of acknowledging the bits of me i disliked
the most that were holding me back.

accepting that change doesn't come in bundles and
letting my weaknesses evolve into something better
became my un-asked for strength. and i wonder
what i would have done if i didn't have these flaws to
complete me.

{excerpt from my diary}

FACADE

I admire people who buy a ticket last minute and decide to escape to another place, people who lodge in lofts and drink coffees from any shop they see. I like to see the look on their faces while they're busy admiring the world when the rest scurry to get to another place.

What is this place we're constantly running to? I have often wondered and 'right here' never seems to be good enough. Perhaps it is our imaginations that have consumed our ability to think rationally. After all, wasn't this what we had run away for yesterday?

I commend people who have the courage to proclaim their love on streets, unaware of whosoever sees them. People who let themselves express instead of hiding the insatiable desire for love running loose within them.

Does love exist? I mean if it did, then I wouldn't have stared blankly at his face while he confessed wanting to spend the rest of his life with me, if I knew I would have trusted the words he had entwined so carefully.

I respect those who are still chasing their passion. Optimistic, that one day it's the struggle that will make them smile. It will be the art created from scraped paint and broken brushes. Loose guitar strings will bear witness for the days spent on streets, selling records with confidence that their music is a form of therapy.

Why do people never take the time to realize their hobbies? I used to think that people with spare time were the only ones running after antique stores and used books.

While I take the time to observe the people around me, I become aware of the fact that while all are busy crossing the street, that none takes a minute to look at another. And I begin to question if we're all hiding a story that reveals the facade we've designed so intricately.

RUNNING INTO YOU IN HALLWAYS

Sitting at the back of classrooms
jotting down my thoughts in science journals
wearing glasses large enough to hide my face
and hair tied back
so they don't mess with the rush of ideas occurring
suddenly in my mind

the sound of school bell
at the end of the hour
has a certain ring to it
but when he stops me in the hallway
asking 'how've you been?'
my stomach turns into a knot

and i don't know
if the nervousness of running into him
scared he'll notice my voice shaking
counts as 'i've been doing good'
with his friends waiting a few steps behind
i wonder if he too had spent time phrasing his words
or will i go back to my room today
and write this event in a hundred different ways.

STILL THINKING ABOUT YOU

It's been awhile since I have met someone who wanted to talk with me for days, like you used to. When I trace back the events that led me to your addiction, I wonder if it was I who approached a friendship gesture, or my loneliness, which had begged for affection in any way possible. I remember you asking me to stay longer on the phone, and I grow uncertain whether it was my voice you adored listening to or the words I would string together - to explain how my day had been? The pictures of your childhood self are still saved in my phone and as much as I wish I had the courage to delete them, sometimes I think how wonderful of a conversation starter they'd be. But I know you've grown older, and I'm sure my adoration for you holds no fascination.

After the years we've spent apart, I wonder if you'd still be interested to know how I've spent the whole day thinking about you.

DID YOU FORGET SOMETHING?

Those words you said were beautiful.
when you went,
you left them behind,
imprinting them into my memory.

I've convinced myself: I HAVE MOVED ON.

But some days i still feel an excruciating beat,
within my ribs
 —

a desire to confront you
if any of them were true
for if they meant so much,
why did you leave them behind?

DID YOU EVER LOVE ME?

I want to ask you things i'm afraid will push you
away.
weather you missed me when the nights got long.
did you think about me when resembled i,
the way i said your name.

Did you repeat it off your tongue,
trying to remember what it sounded like or
if you wrote it next to yours,
to see what it would like if we were together.
occasionally,
i'd dare ask why you left and
if you'd ever come back
if we had a chance,
would you give us a chance if time was in our favor.
do you stare at a blank page,
attempting to write me your feeling
i know you'd never proclaim?
i'd ask you with a mumbling voice
and chattered teeth,
and hiding away a tear;
did you ever love me?

GUT FEELING

I'm hesitant to think about
the first day i approached you,
doubtful,
if i should ever
trust my gut feeling again.

SILHOUETTE

It's a blistering hot afternoon
when i see a silhouette beside me;
with a chalk, i sketch its outline on the pavement
it moves along with me,
mocking me –

As i try to recall its shape
but the shadow i drew is left behind
and the one beside me is of a different shape
when the sun goes down,
this too will disappear
and i begin to ask myself
why i ever needed an abstract presence
to begin with.

CRACKED VOICES AND WISE MEN

Just because you have experienced it, hearing your struggle will not romanticize the pain for others. It might assure them that it eventually works out. Though from time to time, these people are not asking for anyone to correct their mistakes, they don't want you to tell them the easier way, they don't ask for your advice. Just someone hearing them out can make them fly safer. Sometimes all they need is a person to hold their hand - a presence assuring that everything will be fine. Not the assurance of your wisdom, the calmness of your silence would align the cracks in their voices.

TIME

I haven't been feeling content lately
and i'm not sure what has changed
i look the same in my photos and the clothes fit me
the same
i've remained in touch with the people i met two
years ago
but it feels as if a part of me is missing
is this the structure of time?
It takes away a part of you
you never knew existed
and when you're able to cry more frequently than
before
you begin to think what it is that you have left
behind
but it doesn't make sense
so as i begin to put the pieces together
through old messages and letters
i realize that
time is currently stealing another piece of mine
while i rummage through memory to find the old.

GROWING UP

You're only 16, don't be disappointed about the concert you 'almost' went to with your friends, there's so much more music in the world and you're more than that one night of neon lights.

If you're 18 and crying about the boy who broke your heart, pick yourself up and look around you. You'll see so many who care about you and you're more than one boy's rejection.

If you're 19 and regretting that you didn't apply to that one university your parents had insisted on. Let that thought leave you, education is the people you interact with and the humble decisions you learn to make as each day passes by to teach you a lesson, giving you a new opportunity. You're more than the label on your cover letter.

When you're 25 and looking for an apartment, remember it's not going to be view from your penthouse window that'll make the day bearable, keep the loved ones close to you and remember you're more than just a location you tell your friends about.
As you're growing into your thirties, be proud of who you were a decade ago because you will rave about it in your forties. I hope you make it to your sixties. In case the passage of time makes the scenery dull, pick yourself up for the concert you missed 'at that time, in that place' and never regret the moments time was unable to collect for you; because as you grow older you'll realize that it's only going to be yourself keeping it all together and you'll never blame time for getting you so far.

JEALOUSY

I don't understand why the human heart feels like a failure when someone it knows receives an accomplishment. And it's not the trophy, certificates or the accolades that create a barrier from their friendship in front of their eyes; but, the mere thought that they weren't able to achieve the same task.

How a moment of someone's celebration make us feel like the most broken person who exists and why can we not create our own version of happiness?

We must learn to be content in dim lights, when no one is looking. We should be able to tell proudly about the green light we almost missed - without a hint of regret. We must announce that we are *still* waiting for the most thrilling event of our lives to happen, but that we are waiting. And we can wait together.

After all, life isn't supposed to be a race, all of us come and go at a different time.

CAGE

We are not living in a cage
i know we have been informed of the scarcity of time
the vicious cycle of regret that follows
but the time is not moving away from us
we need not fight.
It's moving with us
holding us in place,
making sure that we let ourselves be.
Time is not a demon
we need to capture
it's a flow
moving along with our series of breath
for some it lasts longer
while waiting for a train
and others it whizzes by
like an artist adoring his muse
but time will not trap us
in the confinement of our thoughts
it will lead us to wherever we command it to
it is a result of the ideas in our heads
the feelings in our hearts
the adrenaline in our veins
and time will become a part of us
if we acknowledge its presence in the room right now
because time has still not slipped away from us.

STAY

I was flattered when you asked me to *'stay'*
your voice getting a bit higher towards the end
leaving it as a question mark
as if it were a choice
but i didn't know
someone else could say the same word
and hold me in one place.

FOOTSTEPS

We take steps too loud,
with our feet dragging dust
and shoulders carrying –
a burden of hurt
the soil wasn't created to devour sadness,
its purpose was to bring a home
to someone's existence

yet –

we stomp our feet,
to prove it is the fragile one of both.

BELONG

I have a desire to belong,
in the serenity of my thoughts.

REACHING HOME TO YOU

Should i ever prefer to travel alone,
it will be to reach home to you.

EXPECTATION

Be good, to yourself and the people with you. Share your story about the inspiring person you met on the plane that one time or the new neighbor who moved in across the street last week. Talk about the good friend who taught you the life lesson, saved at the back of your head till this day. People our good and they will remain this way until you expect them to be. So, say, that people are kind and take part in glorifying kindness. Realize that the common enemy between two people is only the expectations they build for each other. And should you be able to shatter this illusion, you'll see that everyone is alike – carrying the same expectations – hoping that the next person they meet will be the kind gesture that the universe had promised them.

WHAT DO YOU WANT TO BE WHEN YOU GROW UP?

Even as a child i didn't know the answer to *"what do you want to be when you grow up?"* I recall no hint of excitement as my brother shouted 'pilot' looking up to the sky, while down below i was struck with a daunting feeling of crashing into the ground.

As the question was repeated, directed towards me again – I'd consider their eyes and ask, *"what do you mean?"* Baffled as they'd be because it was a common question every child should have been accustomed to, I should have had an automated response. They would kindly offer me a list of choices … teacher, pilot, doctor. Sadly, that wasn't the answer my childhood mind was looking for.

While the question remained the same, I began to string better and more words together – yet I didn't have an answer, so I would ask. *"how old do you mean by grow up?"* The answer to that would be, *"you know when you're bigger and stronger"*, at the time the answer only disappointed me but now it astounds me as to how child-like a response I was given with the expectation of providing them with a monosyllabic answer.

So, is it really my fault that I am still searching for an answer?

A PART OF ME

Anything you didn't need,
you left behind.
Silly me,
i thought you had taken
a part of me with you.

BONDS WE CREATE

The commonest of traits that allow people to form a bond is through storytelling. We recall memories, foolish mistakes or commendable pranks. Hilarious, when our stories overlap! Often, if we're lucky, we want this bond to stay. Therefore, more stories must be told. We hunt through incidents about our friends and families - people who've left an impact on our hearts, perhaps even created an imbalance of emotions. But we admire them for the bond we have with them and we wish for a new one too. As our stories begin to transition from funny, to embarrassing, to hurtful and even to our aspirations - we grow skeptic of the bond we are forming. It sounds too good to be true! We get scared of the transparency we might be creating - we doubt that we've become predictable. So we retract parts of stories, embellishing with a few details that become apparent on our faces as we speak. How many times will we hold back until we're secure that this bond will stay?

YOU FEEL SO CLOSE TO ME

Often i catch myself breaking a promise
that i'd never think of you again
i won't imagine your silhouette
before turning off my bedside lamp
i won't hear your voice
in a stranger's foreign accent
but when it's not my mind
rushing off to the corners of your warmth
my heart traces itself
into the silence
it took so long for me to create.

DISTANCE

I've tried pinpointing the exact day we grew apart, but each time learnt that it wasn't within our control. I wondered if it was my fault for replying to your goodbye so quickly or weather you took big steps – trying to blame the distance on something tangible – something we could touch and see and somewhere we could be. Just so we could know exactly what to change if we were given another lifetime.

But I know that was the lifetime we had been promised. Of bent hearts and whispered words, spoken softly into our ears and chuckles of laughter that could not be justified.

Sharing a warm coffee without gloves and no shade to hide us from the pouring rains or the cold December winds which left scars on our cheeks; because, nothing could compare to the shivers down our spines, we felt in each other's presence.

It was a forever we had thought of promising but who knew that memory could have a hold so strong, that each day felt like a lifetime with you gone. I thought of blaming the brutal July summers that would melt our ice creams and create a puddle of sweet milk on the street. But it's the clinking of coins against your wristwatch as you took out pennies to pay the ice-cream man that I remember.

When I looked at you for the first time and shared a smile, I realize that this is what the silence had promised us. The distance. So cruelly, reminding us of what it felt in our bones when we were together. If it weren't for the distance, what else would we have thought of at the mention of our names?

WHERE WOULD YOU LIKE TO MEET?

Say, we run into each other years from now, where would you want it to be?

Perhaps the broken benches near the train station; in the town home to both of us, or at the top of the bakery roof we shared our music, during one of our little rendezvous. I don't know if your mp3 still carries the same loud, penetrating music we'd dance to so joyously. Makes me smile and laugh at our attempt at ballroom dance to such discordant beats.

But if you don't remember anything after all this time, would you want it to be in a mall, bustling with people so we'd have no choice but to end our meeting abruptly. Or maybe a park so the many age groups can bear witness to that we can stand still together. But i don't know if time will make you shy or crowds will still threaten my personal space. Somehow, my mind reaches out to the streets of London; where red buses create a color on the streets despite the confused feelings of its inhabitants. Perhaps it's the promise of a cold weather – swooning us into a warm coffee shop. And I wonder if the smell of freshly crushed cocoa beans will take you back to my mother's kitchen where we tried baking chocolate cookies for the first time. I remember that we had forgotten about the timer and the cookies burnt, and the smell of fresh cocoa beans is incomparable but isn't this what memory is all about? It takes you back into a bizarre time lapse. However, I'm afraid if we utter *'how've you been?'* at the same time, the answer will become invalid and we'd have jinxed it all. And I wonder if it'd be suitable to mention the moments we had already spent together, for who knows we might have made better memories to share.

LET'S TRAVEL THE WORLD

Let's travel the world together!

What occurs in my mind are a series of
gorgeous,
carved out places,
soaked in history and culture and languages
that cascade beyond the oceans.

My first thought is that i'm walking,
with a camera in hand,
trying to capture everything –
trees bending from age,
the smell of basil on fresh pizza,
puddles of rain that everyone seems to avoid but us.

To capture, you and i,
seeing it all from the far corner through our
kaleidoscope.
the thrill of looking over these pictures,
weeks from now
entices me to create a bond with wherever i am.

But really, what i mean today
is for us to know each other completely.
the language of our laughter and grief,
how the two complement each other but never
correlate.
When we return tired from a long day,
our minds to remember which side of the bed
belongs to whom.
Forgive all that we forgot to pack,
This is enough.

Another day.

This is the journey i asked for.

WHEN YOU NEXT MEET

Months passed by –
    when you met her again
    she waved a little *"hi"*
    catching you by surprise.

All you could do –
    stare until it got a little awkward
    and before you could muster a smile
    she had looked the other way.

GIRL LIKE ME

You've found an exciting lover,
who cares if you forgot to say goodbye
i'm sure you thought i'd be
where you had left me off to be.

After all –
it's not difficult
to get over a girl like me.

FORGET ME

I wish –
that you forget me
forget that someone loved you
so much that infinity would burst into shatters.

I hope –
my presence fades
for if it were in our tragic fate
i wouldn't have it this way.

I pray –
your heart doesn't hurt
at the mention of my name
i oh so know how it feels.

Forgetting me would be so sensational,
i wish i could do the same.

HOPE

If in this life,
you really do end up searching for hope –
be sure to not look too far,
so at least you'll know it's within your reach.

GRANDPARENTS

If the next time, you receive a handwritten letter in a wrinkled envelope, containing a birthday wish and a feeble request of a visit – don't let it go. Our grandparents have an amiable quality of watching over us, from afar. A unique seventh sense that is always able to sense something is wrong by a simple touch on the shoulder. It used to be impressive when we were 8 year olds, running around their house, hoping we'd get to build a tree house any day. But as we grew years, this quality began to intimidate us – scared that we'd give in too much, so it became safer to maintain distance.

But how is it, that when their hug embraces us, a thousand childlike feelings emerge within and we forget what to say beyond the *'i've missed you'* that escapes our mouths automaticallyIt isn't the first time but when we see them eating food without a screen lit in front, it baffles us. We realize it has been far too long since we enjoyed a meal without the presence of a T.V screen. As we try to blame this on their age, convincing ourselves that time will do this to us one day; we don't recall the electrifying feeling as we play frisbee in the backyard together. That rush of commitment to run to the other end of the yard despite the soiled t-shirt and bruised knees doesn't jog back to memory again. And as we try to remember this feeling, we realize that we have yet again missed out on a story that our grandparents are telling with an amiable smile.

Looking at grandmother's smoky gray hair and grandfather's goatee, we realize that we had heard this one before but missed out on the lesson they'd been ending it off on. That high note, which was meant to inspire our childhood self but we had always dozed off before the story ended.

How pleasant is it to recall all these faded
sentiments, in another time frame – to realize that
an angelic presence had been striving to teach us
simplicity all along. And what a wonderful
combination it makes, with our parents trying to give
us all.

DON'T CHANGE

Another year is ending
a large commemoration –

it always had been

dancing,
group photos,
looking ahead to new resolutions
promising ourselves *something* will get better.

I'm afraid i never knew what that *something* was –
that i had prayed for so long and hard
but i know it came and passed
or if not,
it was eventually going to come and go.

As i flip over
folded corners of my yearbook photos,
i notice that *'don't change'* has been signed
way too many times.

I'm afraid, this year too –
another leaf has fallen off a tree,
yet it all seems the same.

THE BIRD

The years, scattered around a calendar
are proclaiming the country's freedom
i wonder which empty space
on this piece of paper
will become a reminder
of the shackles i have tangled around myself

perhaps it will be the job,
i am still not old enough for
or the financial freedom
which will ring bells
and open the space
i have reserved in my heart,
for the day it'll skip a beat
and i'll know that i need not
stay in one place
for the rest of my life

but chains are only an expression
for the walls we build around ourselves

<pre>
                                        height
                                  certain
                              a
                        to
                    up
              flies
          bird
      a
even
</pre>

the day i learn to express myself
i'll understand the bird had taken flight
only to know –
if it's feathers could keep it warm.

HAUNTED HOUSE

When you visited an amusement park
did you too
leave the haunted house till the last?
as if you knew
that the tingling sensation under your feet
justified it'd be exhilarating
expecting something to grab your feet
afraid you'll jump into another trap
but you know that the darkness was only created
so the led lights could confuse your path.

But scared that –
the thrill of the roller coasters
and joy from the teddy bears
that you'd win on your hundredth turn
won't seem as exciting,
that the splash from the water slides
won't be loud enough
to dull the screeching noises.

And if you bumped into someone
you'd instantly scream
followed by laughter
that no one would tell you is too loud
because all will be finding
something to hold onto
they know isn't real.

START AGAIN

Loving the way her hair followed the breeze
she'd wander off to know
if it led to somewhere
chasing the path it had travelled
before reaching her

she didn't stay
in one place,
refusing to settle down
to the calmness
of a life lived on *repeat*

and i always wondered
if it said about her commitment
or
of the courage she had
to start again.

THE CONCEPT

If this is how i am to remain forever
held in one spot
with a mind wandering off
to places i haven't heard to exist
or people destined to remain strangers.

> *adamant to climb a mountain one day,*
> *i'm convincing myself to stop crying.*

Nothing created were meant to be broken
but each with a purpose, to fulfill
and i thought that tears would claim me fragile
but even the sky pours it heart out
on a surface, below
it is unsure of existing.

And when the rain drops
onto a pavement
with tattered cracks
and creeping moss
moist leaves
which have been trodden upon
our only response is that
it fell from heaven.

So i hope –
even if my heart is not as vast as the sky
or has the silver lining
my mother thinks reflects through my eyes
i know that, i too
am as fragile and strong
as the rain drops pelting, furiously
but remembering it's concept –
to heal the barren,

the thirsty.

S L O W   M O T I O N

In s l o w m o t i o n
i flipped a coin
it didn't go as far up
as i always imagined it did.

Mesmerized in its motion,
tracking the heads and the tails,
counting how many times
the coin will take a 360 turn
before falling on the ground
and rolling towards the far end
where i will have to run - to catch up.

Before i have reached –
with a panting breath
and eyes fixated
on a small piece of metal
which may or may not
take another turn
or fall,
the coin stops rolling.

I learn that the s l o w m o t i o n
had not promised me constant time intervals
and i still can't tell,
if it landed on heads or tails
or what was that i had bet on.

MY HOUSE

If i get the chance to live on long enough
for someone to call me wise
i yearn to tell them things will not always work out
but it's okay you believed they would

you can draw a tiny house –
with a yellow sun in the corner of the page,
paint the roof brick red,
place a blue car next to a tree,
remember to draw a smile on the boys' and girl's
faces

this will be your work of art
and it deserves a place on the wall
as this drawing is replaced with another
you'll start to wonder why
the windows were always closed

inside, there might be two lonely people
with an insatiable desire to get over with the day
i must tell them some nights
they'll cry themselves to sleep
and the next day will still carry its memory

although very soon, between now and then
while the clouds above the house remain blue
a time would have passed by
making the memory a part of itself
and you'll start to wonder why
you only drew the front view of this house.

CHAOS

The taps ran in front of her
as she brushed her teeth
with a sequence of backwards and forwards motion
scrutinizing her reflection in the mirror,
she noticed the moon-shaped birthmark, which was
always there

   noticeable

      yet hidden

near the edge of her nose
she started to feel guilty for the water she had left
running
flowing all too quickly
worried, she'd run out of hot water
and her father would scream through the other room
waiting for her to dress herself
        was she getting late?
the alarm hadn't gone off yet
yet the tick tock
was audible at the back of her head
intently, she looked at her teeth
which were glistening all too white
but her arms couldn't stop the motion
three minutes
that's how she had done it since age five
three minutes
perhaps, it had been longer,
she brushed a few more strokes
just to be sure
gargling with the fresh water
before she turned off the taps
and the chaos would pause
until the *three minutes*
it'd repeat on, tomorrow.

MORE OR LESS

Would you be all right?
if nothing you ever wished for
comes true...

along the embankments
of a parched river,
where seaweeds dangle,
on its surface
a contrast of green,
providing –
tainted reflections
dotted with dust

would it be able to convince you
that once it carried
more life
and less courage
but now the two –
could not exist together
and so they
switched their places?

THIS IS IT

We are all going to fall
and we all get to choose how.

FAILURE

I am not a failure
if i can recall
my mistakes,

and i am not a failure –
if my voice doesn't crack
while listing them out loud.

THAT DAY

I dread the day
you'll say
you've missed me
because
then i'll know
i had been
on your mind
this whole time.

A LITTLE PRAYER

Pray,

that i start existing in my thoughts
along with the rest –

which hides so calmly,
and screams in silence,
that –

which was never meant to exist.

NIGHT

What is the first thing that comes to your mind when you hear the mention of *night*? Many of us are bombarded with a spur of negative connotations - dark, scary, dangerous or all of the above. When on a road, we keep our gazes straight towards the path and stride towards our destination, not looking elsewhere too much – in case someone gets suspicious. And when we see our neighbors' front lights off, we wonder if it's because they haven't been home or simply forgotten. As a motorcycle whizzes by, our only thought is that someone is in a hurry and someone is reaching home. Silently, we pray in our hearts that they reach safe. Perhaps, that's why the moon and stars were created – to guide us home – to show us light while we hide beneath a blanket, terrified of even a leg escaping the safe comfort of the little confinement we create for ourselves; assured that keeping our knees close to our chests and snuggling with a pillow would somehow keep us safe.

But I wonder for a little while, that I could only – I was only able to see the stars after scrutinizing at the dark sky for so long that my iris stayed fixated and could not adjust itself easily when I shook my head, and stared at the streetlight, making up for the darkness I thought I had taken too much of. And do you worry about the kids, who are made to fall asleep at the mere thought of a monster pouncing from underneath their beds?

We wake up abruptly – in the middle of the night, when one of the windows get closed by the cool night air, whose only purpose was to bring the scent of evening primroses to our windowsill, awakening us to witness its blossom.

If we notice someone sitting alone on a balcony, with
smoke puffs creating a grey screen in front of their
faces – making it difficult for us to recognize if we've
seen them before, our only impression is that they're
lonely. We forget that a nightingale is singing its
nocturnal song, somewhere - at the same time we
keep our eyes shut – convinced we'll fall asleep any
minute now.

When empty streets, closed windows and sirens from
an ambulance at a place too far from here – can
create an impression of comfort, I'll be convinced
that day and night were created to exist in harmony;
for the only cowards are the one's associating 2.00
am with the dawn of a new day.

GETTING READY

Blue jeans, folded from the bottom
a crease for each fold
and each fold to precision
right above her ankles
to avoid it coming into her feetdespite the velvety
curls,
she tied her hair back,
a black hair-tie –
tied into a pony

chap stick in her side pocket
she let the cuff buttons close,
click

brown leather,
bought in salea backpack on her shoulder,
something she knew
would never grow old
if not, she'll call it vintage

a bottle, a diary, a phone
a checklist ran through her mind

slipped on her favorite flats
clueless, if it'd be a demanding day
or one where she sits all day,
wondering what she had forgotten today

keys slipped from her hands
into her pocket
and pulled the door shit behind
with a day still yet to begin
why, did she so calmly
prepare for the worse?

MANABI

My first job came in 9th grade when I began tutoring a five years old girl. Manabi lived two streets away and came on a bicycle with her father and everyday she'd take off her pink helmet decorated with stickers, ruffle her hair, before sending me the warmest smile which could ever compliment crooked teeth and a tongue stained with orange juice. Twice a week, we'd learn alphabets and numbers, something which were on the top of my tongue; but, watching the young girl struggle made me wonder if I too had had difficulty pronouncing the number *seven*. Weather I too replaced the v with a b and if I too, used to count on my toes after I ran out of fingers to count on. But all of this only seems like an observation from a person who is unknown to the struggles of a five-year-old – constantly waiting for another year to pass, impatient to get older, as if each birthday fulfilled wishes of mythical super powers. Manabi taught me to laugh if I forgot the spelling of a *bee* or if I lost count and had to start again, she taught me how wonderfully simple it is to begin again. She was a proof of that it's okay to climb the stairs one step at a time, and it wasn't a problem if sometimes you had to look down at your feet to see where you were walking.

With years left in between, my next job was as an intern. Dressed in button shirts and closed shoes, everything here was in a different language. Although systematic, the processes were more tedious and as much as I appreciated a good working machine, the fascinations of a 5-year-old were unparalleled to the creativity sessions and group meetings that attempted their *light bulb moment*.

After that, when there wasn't enough money in jars
labeled *university, travel* and *shopping* - I took to the
solace of minimum wage. And as I stood there,
bagging jams and milk bottles in brown paper bags,
waiting for the clock to tick another hour – my ears
would hear her little voice, *"are we finished yet?"*
Eyes looking intently into mine with the kind of
confidence we wish we carried growing up and a
smile that could not be justified. It has seemed to me
that the lessons and moments spent at my first job
will continue to resonate and find traces of it in any
other opportunity I find myself in. If not, I'll hold on
meekly to an intricately crafted corporate ladder,
reminding myself – there had always been enough to
support me.

A PROPOSAL

I spent today thinking about the first boy who first proclaimed his affection for me. In early August, when the falling of rust leaves rolled out a carpet for the beginning of a new school year – my eyes were focused on the new shoes I had bought for myself, careful, not to let any dust settle on the new surface.

I took each step cautiously which later you'll describe to be *graceful*, but I'm afraid I had tripped over in my mind several times before you approached me and I couldn't recall your name. You didn't begin the conversation with my name, because now I understand, your voice would have shaken more and it is only the trembling of your hands which you were to later justify to your friends. With a chocolate in hand, you proposed me the title of being your girlfriend but i had not run this relationship in my head before, so before there was time to negotiate a friendship; i turned down the chocolates and walked away, with a group of boys looking down on me. I was laid with guilt when I questioned my response; but my 13-year-old self could not understand the reason for this blunt response.

I suppose I only wanted to know what a lover would do. That's why when you told me *"it's either you or no one"*, my heart fluttered and I must have paused my nervous banter to understand the meaning of words I had only heard in movies. With such courage in your voice, it could not have masked the insecurities I think I was born with. I supposed you must have noticed the hesitation in my eye- liner because at the age of 13 I was only a nervous wreck, and I was not ready for words like yours. But even at the age of 13, I wanted to know how long you'd stay, before you'd had too much of me; so I suppose it only took a mumbled *no* from me for you to run over to my best friend and I suppose you never noticed the question mark I had left hanging at the end.

MRS. SOMEONE'S LAST NAME

"You don't have to try", I was told when I put on too much mascara and my blush was not just a reflection of the color of my dress. Some days I'd look at the pictures of my friends – notice the girls they took photographs with. An arm around her torso and pursed lips indicating a burst of laughter, any moment to follow the camera clicked and I wondered if I'd be a girl next to a boy who would shift several times, just for the perfect picture. A part of me questioned if this perfect picture was meant to be stacked in a kitchen drawer, something to look back on while eating our morning cereal or just so it could be taken, for the sake of a fleeting moment.

I didn't have to try, but the nights I couldn't fall asleep, my mind would wander off to suicidal thoughts of a perfect guy. His face never distinguishable, but his broad shoulders and a perfect jawline – only makes me look for him in every boy. I wonder why he wears a suit, and I still can't tell why I'm always sitting on a comfortable grey recliner and an interior heating system warming the soles of my feet as i walk towards him – and that's it, I fall asleep and I wish that I could have stayed up longer, be able to see his face – to find him in a crowd.

So one day, when I bought a corset from a sale where good girls shopped from, the shopkeeper asked why I was buying it. I didn't have a Cinderella ball to go to, neither was I a cover girl. No one had guided me to tie the strings of this old- fashioned clothing, and it went into several knots – a few of which never came undone, I wondered if I'd eventually have to cut myself loose but *I had kept trying.*

I think *I was still trying* when I subconsciously
prayed for him in front of any place of worship.
Basilica, temple, mosque, church – afraid someone
would ask my religion and whispering *'him'* wouldn't
be enough. Alas! In introducing him, I learnt I had
only a name, given at birth without my consent to
show for my identity. *So I'll keep trying* to construe
adjectives and illustrate my character description
before I strive to fit his brief – of a name next to his -
lying in one statement.

FALLING

now,
   i am
      falling
         recklessly
but i shouldn't be, i think to myself
inside my head is a voice, like always
asking if it was the risk i had finally taken

but i don't take risks –
i walk along sidewalks
and tip toe on outlines
marked with chalks, laying boundaries
with labels, warning
and constant alarms, ringing

this time i can't blame gravity for
      pulling
         me
           down
maybe here, i meet the demons in my head
the one's who shout are hidden, but imminent
should i look up to see if the clouds resemble a
fleece?

but i'm keeping an eye –
for the surface underneath
and looking up
will only remind me
of how far i have gotten from there
with no place to fit "here"

if only there was a parachute
to balance the forces against me
it doesn't feel right
that my second chance,
only feels like the first.

BABY BROTHER

———

I took my first step the day my parents brought
home a baby brother for me; he lay in a crib and I
reached towards him, with my tiny wobbly legs and
arms spread out to balance my movement. From
that day, my parents thought I were to conquer a
world – funny, they didn't know my adventurous
inhibitions would only dare me to run away with a
boy – a mistake – later to justify with *"we were just a
couple of kids"*. I must have had a lot to say, when I
heard my brother cry and all I could do was cry in
response, attracting my father to see what was
happening. When he held him in his lap, I'd finally
stop crying and get on playing with my blocks,
creating the tallest building possible, little did I know
the height of this building depended on the number
of blocks I had or how tall I could stand in front of it,
before my arms fell short to reach the top. And when
he was put in a baby chair, and I was allowed to sit
on the table; along with the big kids, I didn't know
whether it meant I was capable of eating on my own
or that I had been trusted, with the responsibility of
sitting still on my own – able to differentiate a fork
from a spoon. I cried out loud, for the chair my baby
brother sat in, where I'd feel comfortable on the
reliance of someone else feeding me. Ironic, now I
hear, it is the older sibling who sets an influence.

———

•

(DOT)

Nothing feels scarier than the prospect of running out of words to say. Despite the books resting on your bookshelves, or the many stacks of ink-stained paper – belonging from the nights when you attempted to pen down your feelings – things you've promised never to let anyone know. But grocery and bucket lists aren't enough to give you the assurance that you'll conquer the forces holding you back. Forces that make us believe that the life of an average person on an average ought to be more than just simple. Forces that make you believe you'll never be able to phrase your feelings, and the commemoration speeches will always remain reserved for those who appear taller on the stage.

Our teachers had used a magic wand to teach us how to turn alphabets to words to sentences to paragraphs, but never did they show us the magic potion that created clouds of glitter, as its lid was unscrewed.

Our creative license was kept hidden in the bottom drawer of their desk, where we always imagined a red apple sitting, calmly. They told us that an intelligent student ended their sentences with a dot; a list carried commas and exclamation marks were an indication of something dramatic. We ought to resort to it, as our last alternative. One meant that we were scared, two was a signal of utter attention and three exclamation marks were only used by the brave kids – the outcasts, the one who played with punctuation and took grammar as a joke, so we held ourselves back. After all, who wants to be made fun of in a 4th grader's classroom?

———

We restricted ourselves to short phrases and carefully drew small circles, filling them in with our pencils – which always required an extra sharpening and never made it to the end of it, unlike the sentences which were always marked with a beginning and an end.

This is how we were taught to keep silent in a classroom, bustling with children who had had a sugar rush the night before, and how beautifully this carried on with us outside a room that held so much to say.

•

SHIPWRECK

I pulled the rope to set the triangular white sail high, smiling proudly when it rested against the wind. With the Archimedes principle set on repeat in my head, I took hold of the steering gear strongly and sailed aboard. I kept a copy of the hands-on sailing instructions in my front pocket and looked straight ahead – praying there will be plenty of light in the sky before I reach the shore. I looked at the map, exactly how I had been promised and trained, with an abstract picture in mind. With accolades hanging in my bedroom and the stack of certificates resting in my father's office, I was certain I'd make them proud again. If navigation turned out as planned, I should be able to deliver the valedictorian speech i had written 4 years ago. 3as the sail beat into the wind, I looked in closely to notice the sail was not lifting towards the side with lower pressure – my ship would cease to move soon. With a heartbeat running on thousand nautical miles a second, I recalled Newton's laws and frantically ran across the ship, wondering if the hull and keel were creating the unwanted resistance. I hadn't been prepared for this, the shore was bound to be nearby but before I could look around, I found myself in pitch-black darkness. Unsure, if I were still living my eyes adjusted to the dark green and blue ocean pulling me towards it. Remembering how to breathe, I searched for the predators who were meant to arrive in shoals and a skeleton of unknown specie to tell me I'd never arrive on the sheltered island. Finally accepting, this is how it was going to be, I set to look around the deep ocean – wondering where the underwater mines were located. "Can you sniff gold?" I questioned as the coral reefs appeared before me, set in caves of their own. Colors I had seen before but of a different intensity - an unfamiliar color palette. Seashells rested gracefully on the surface, allowing small fishes to rest nearby.

Transparent jellyfishes created blobs of light amidst darkness, contracted their bodies and used their tentacles to propel against the same forces which had sunk me - their upwards motion, showing the way out.

As I reached to the surface, gasping for air. The wooden barks floated on the surface - a memory of a voyage. Wishing something similar would happen again, so I could find my own way back.

TO MY LONG DISTANCE FRIEND,

Moving place to place surely portrays the temporariness of certain aspects of our lives – how easily we adjust to a new grocery store, learning each aisle name from second day onwards, that 50% off sales posters only require for you to notice the bold numbers, ignoring all the rest in a different language, which you have only now seen to exist; justifying that people have more in common than a traveler believes.

We shop in different currencies but I still convert it to see whether you'd accept a present in case I went past our set limit. We may have changed whom we share our drinks with but our love for mango shakes and swirly straws has remained the same. And postcards have remained regular, featuring your new friends – the people taking most of your time now and I do the same – often adding an inside joke in the post script which I'm sure you still notice. My roommate knows my schedule from dawn to dusk, she even shares her toothpaste when I run out of mine – isn't this what we had said a good friend would do? When she falls asleep early, I don't mind shutting off my laptop screen, adhering to we'd both have a good sleep and maybe one day, she'll do the same for me. But it was only you who who'd ring my phone until I woke up, because your neighbor had parked in your spot again and needed me to help you shout at him again. I have still kept your pictures in my phone and you probably have the same one' s too because we made sure to share them; however, I understand that our lock screens must carry a captured moment with different people who are in our lives now – we agreed that friends ought to be a support system and agreed to respect anyone who'd approach us with a friendship gesture.

I admire how are friendship never
restricted us from creating new connections, despite
the half-broken hearts we wear around our wrists
and people wonder if it's for you or for the boy who
broke my heart. So I just laugh it off, leaving the
question to be answered by you – in another letter
that you'll write me because aren't you sitting there
in a different time zone with a pen in hand, thinking
where to start from – finding traces of me in your
new relationships?

This time, I write to you to thank you for
making *distance* sound like an element, poets only
write about.

Love,
Your BFF <3

COUNTDOWN

If you ever see me on a t.v show,
it won't be on a talk show or a live interview,

flip between channels
starring athletes and singers
and pull the volume up when you see
so your living room captivates the same atmosphere
as on the stage, where the host is waiting for my
answer
10,
9,
8,
i'd probably be biting my lower lip
staring blankly at the audience
7,
6,
praying that god will send me a sign
so i choose the right box,
promising a jackpot
5,
you'll notice the impatient host,
giving me a glare
i am taking too long, but
the question seemed to have a twist
5 seconds left: someone will shout
i'll begin to wonder how long it had been
and if it took longer than it should have
4,
3,
will these 3 seconds pass slower?: my mind will drift
off
it will seem like this countdown will go on
till forever has passed – in series of 10 seconds,
2,
1,
making me feel each second as the last.
0.

A LETTER

Once, i attempted writing you a letter,
125 days after you and (i) stopped talking.
it was (meant) to be pages
carrying adoration (for) our time together,
an attempt to make (you) nostalgic –
but when it started with
"do you want (to) try again?"
i realized you'd keep it down,
after the only sentence i could (write).
so this letter sits beside (me) in an envelope,
torn apart, with jagged edges (too) –
a reminder that i didn't even
have the courage to let this go.

DREAM CATCHER

I have developed a temporary crush
for the object hanging on my wall
its loose intricate web,
and feathers decorating
a willow hoop

fragile –

       no, my dreams are not!

so i use a thicker thread
tighten the strings
and cut feathers out of card

how would the good and bad dreams
even find their way
to my sleeping self
when i have stayed awake all night
crafting each dream catcher?

of a different size and color –
there are too many to hold,
not enough space on the walls
i am counting, only to find
i have not created enough.

WHAT WILL I DO TODAY

The smoky fragrances of incense and soft glows from candle-lit lamps have been unknown to my bedroom interior. I bought a lot of things – from garage sales, discount stores, occasionally from shops with glass windows; but none of the objects were ever meant to correlate with the other. once, I wanted a monochrome setting, with a painting above my bed and since then, a frame has been tilting to a side, too high up for me to adjust. only thing resembling me are the many posters taped on the walls, their edges overlapping – a cluttered mess. the plant on my window sill forces me to keep the window open, inviting dust to settle onto a pile of books I never bothered building a shelf for. maybe I'll get some polaroid photographs to hang on the wall, with a string of led lights above – creating a shrine of photogenic memories. I pick one up and notice the folded corners and a glossy surface scarred with scratches from the pens and calculators I had shoved near it. it looks aged compared to the fresh color pastels I had bought in vain, and a basketball resting in the far corner – slowly running out of air, probably never to be dribbled again. I have yet to throw away old notebooks whose extra pages I had promised to use but the doodles on science notes are only a reminder of the acidic blotches on lab counters. mark sheets and reports cards have quietly remained folded in a drawer, along with a clutch I intended to use only on special occasions; but, this too has grown weary of being kept in one spot – with no change to follow. finally, I decided to stack my shoes in boxes, they were easy to pair but one of the left feet was missing and so I spent the whole day finding it. a dust bunny flew near my nose

and the tingly sensation followed by blockage of air
left me feeling parched. suddenly, I remembered that
I had forgotten to water the plant today.

PROM QUEEN

First –
we cut crowns out of paper
decorated it with glitter
borrowed a mum's dress
which always came under our feet
pretending it was intended to be.

Then –
a sash that carried our name
with a label that struck
"prom queen 2016"
and the host cried out our name,
confetti entangled our hair
as we raised our hands to wave at the crowd.

Humbly –
we'd repeat this act
with ourselves as the host this time
switching the names around
i know what our mistake was now.

<u>We forgot to reach the stage
after the first had waved her good-bye.</u>

Maybe –
there wasn't meant to be one
but each taking their turns
so the show could go on
isn't this why we had collected
the confetti from the floor?

I'M DONE

I thought i had given myself enough time,
to erase my mind of you,
cleaned every thought that uttered your name
deleted every video clip that appeared in front of my
eyes,
every time i was cooking lunch,

burnt my finger –
cried if the lamb was overcooked
but it was never really the dinner which tasted
empty
it was something i had promised not to mention

i do not create an image of you in my head anymore
the words don't ring like a gong outside a temple
i even wrote your name incorrectly,

a hundred times over, so i'd forget how to spell it
and i do not mention you in my journal

i don't even avoid the places we'd been to

then why do i feel a pain
when i think of falling in love – all over again

because this time i know it will last

this time i know he will stay
this time i'm sure it won't hurt

but i'll still remember the pain.

A STREET

He told me: one day,
i'll name a street after you.

I asked him:
why would you want
everyone walking on a road
that was built
just for you?

STEPPING-STONES

I'm scared of rivers
for it's gushing flow of water
it's ability to sweep everything
all
   at
      once
more than that –
i am terrified of the sea it connects with
where nothing ever comes back from

so i take each step carefully
stepping onto the wobbly stones
unaware of the depth of water

never learned to stay afloat –
but, i admire the swimmers
who have the courage to dive in
all
   at
      once
if only i had the courage to plunge
into the unknown
instead of finding planks of wood,
to support my movement.

BEST STORY

The greatest piece of fiction
will be the story we tell about ourselves.

TREE HOUSE

Remember, as a child we wanted to build a
treehouse?
where our mothers couldn't tell us to clean our
rooms
and our fathers couldn't find us

                                    an escape –

it'd be hidden amongst the leaves
and we'd watch our neighbors dogs
through the binoculars we bought from a toy shop.

we imagined it was build out of strong material,
decorated with velvet cushions
and all our toys sat in one corner
while we jumped from branch to branch,
chasing after a sparrow,

which too was only looking for an escape.

I suppose the secrecy lost its charm
when we asked our parents to buy us some wood,
and teach us how to nail it

plank   to   plank.

And they'd say that the tree isn't strong enough
to hold all the weight,
that we'd fall
the best of all –
you already have a house, what do you need this for?

we went crying into our rooms,
promising we'll grow a huge tree
and let our kids build a tree house one day.

CRITICISM

The more you criticize
the more i fall in love
all i can notice is
you   noticing   me.

I NEED YOU DADDY

Daddy, will you walk me to school today?
i promise, i won't look ashamed
when you hold my hand
my skin crawls when i notice the boys staring
even after i have walked past them
sometimes, i wonder if i'm overthinking –
if only i'd heard you say 'have a good day!'
Maybe my day would have been better

Daddy, i need you –
i can't push through crowds without your help

I'm not as brave as i thought i'd be.

OUR SOCIETY

I think we are the same
as we were decades ago
perhaps it is a feature of history

to repeats itself –

this time it doesn't have a voice
which speaks up for injustice
or begs for freedom

maybe history repeats –

but in a different form
this time disguising itself
as slaves of beauty
and masters of judgment.

BED TIME

I couldn't stay up
the way you liked to
late at night
to watch silent movies
and eat bowls of popcorn

maybe the reason
i used to sleep
was to see if
you'd wake up
just to wish me
a good morning

sitting here today
lying awake at night
has shown me that
the sun will rise
regardless of you
and it was always
up to me
to wake up or not.

LUCK

Certainly –
working hard will bear its results.

But often –
it's pure luck that gets people to places
and i wondered if those who made it
to where they always wanted to be
had deserved to make it that far.

Begging for a miracle –
isn't this what we raise our hands
towards the sky for?
waiting for the strings upstairs
to guide the puppets.

Perhaps –
the people who made it
had faith in something.

miracles,
religion,
or if lucky,

themselves

and the people who didn't –
kept blaming their failure on semantics.

I FEEL NOTHING

sometimes it bothers me how easily
i am able to understand a friend's reason
      when they call up last minute to cancel.
when my boyfriend and i have a fight,
      all i say at the end of it is
      you know what, it's okay
      maybe he had a tough day or
      even worse
      maybe i was frustrated –
      with my job,
because that too was a result of the honors degree
i had failed to achieve.
i hate it that i observe the people around me –
      from their long breaths before a sigh,
      or the wrinkle around their eyes
      that follows a smile,
      how some people scratch their chin
      before delivering difficult news.
should i be worried that my reactions are never
spontaneous?
that i do not leap out of my bed
when i hear the doorbell ring,
a hundred things go through my head –
informing me of the best and worst case scenarios.

how farewell drinks have always been
underwhelming –
because since the day i met them,
      i knew there was bound to be a time
      we'd grow separate ways,
      with that little but not too sparkling hope
      we'll run into each other in places we aspired
to be.
however, not a tear would leave my eyes –
and i hate it how i were never able to justify this.
i wish i wasn't this rational,
      i wish i made a big deal out of everything,

i wish i didn't hide my emotions by living in
other people's shoes.
at least,
then someone might wonder what it's like to
look from my eyes –
how incredibly exhausting it is to feel
nothing and everything – all at once.

ON MY MIND

Always –

hurt had always
been the only inspiration
guiding me to draw your face
on a canvas
with the darkest of colors
an empty canvas waits

on repeat –

i put on the song
which always reminded me of you
hoping it'd disintegrate my heartbeat
on a thousand different frequencies
and i'd pray for it to go away

but no –

i can shout your name
knowing it could be anyone's

i have nothing to complain about
and the song isn't giving me goose bumps
my eyes have not watered
i have fidgeted from my place
more than several times
to know if i feel the same

                i don't know what to do
                without you on my mind.

OFFICE

I am sitting in an office,
with a laptop set in place
people chatting politely –
waiting for the other to stop talking
before they utter a reply.
a nod in between
even a *mhmm*
showing they're on the same page.
as this short conversation ends,
they move back to their seats,
a leg over the other
eyes targeting the screen
some stare blankly
others type furiously,
trying to create a rhythm
that matches with their heartbeat.

After all those years i had spent
worrying in school
if i'd ever make it to this chair,
seem to have been spent in vain –
considering all the mistakes
i thought i had made were fatal,
the results have not been brutal.

I regret the lunch times
i spent creating speeches
for the havoc that were student elections,
here, no one is interested to know
what the other has to say

Who knew –
i had been preparing
for a life set on repeat,
and the calmness
would not make me feel safe.

LISTS

You know how we talk about our aspirations
and the huge

breakthrough, which would transform our lives –
when we sit down on a quiet evening,
jotting down our thoughts
which luckily occur in the right order
the bucket list always sitting in our first drawer
and the sticky notes stuck on our refrigerators.

But it worries me
that if the human nature is immune
to setting a limit for itself,
then why does the list of aspirations
end with the length of the paper
and how come they are not listed
according to our priority
and why does it never state
the activity which would finally
grant us the sense of fulfillment
that after it –
we will finally feel the way we wish to?

WEDDING CRAVINGS

Am I the only girl who hasn't planned her wedding out loud? It never held a charm for me. After all, how could everything I've ever wished form would come from one occasion. It isn't a simple wish...Yet, the dresses and smell of flowers; accompanied with lights and music, flashes before my eyes, when I see a friend walking down the aisle – her flawless smile and eyes looking down to hide away the tears, everyone gushes at how fabulous the arrangements are. As she stands next to the groom, the whole world seems to be set in place and I feel a tingle down my back – craving a presence I do not need. To have an arm around mine, whispering mellifluous words I know I will not remember because I'd be too busy pretending I don't care. I see the night is one in many for the both, but the only thought haunting my frivolous heart is if this one occasion will be enough of a reminder to prove their choice was wise. If not, the flowers would have blossomed in vain – and I know it's normal to take a leap that promises to hold everything in its place. But it's the other part of me, which is blankly questioning the existence of such sentiments that may or may not just be vibes – and once again I've been thinking too much. I suppose I never planned weddings because of its temporariness, like the guests forget the dinner menu and the bride lets go of her gown. How the groom doesn't remember the music playlist he had personalized himself, and the only things that matter were never on display in the room that day. It could be, that it is only a bet – after all, if it doesn't last, how difficult could it be to plan another one, if everything had already been sorted in the head – years ago, when the only words synonymous to cravings were chocolate and ferry rides.

SAD

I feel deflated
and not the kind
where i keeping eating
to fill the emptiness.

SAFE

A part of me feels safe
knowing that no one
understands
or will ever
decipher my emotions
through the black irises
which will only show them
their own reflection

i feel safe
because no one can reason
justify
explain
the way i am
because
complexity is unattractive

so i get to obscure parts of me
and reveal to myself
completely
for i know
how i got the patches on my heart
and scars on my wrist

only i can explain
the long nights
spent awake
that gave me dark circles
and the tired feet
which hold me up

safe –

IN AN INSTANT

Suddenly,
it was time
to start something new
and believe in the magic
of new beginnings.

THE VIOLIN

Standing near the music stand
with no music sheets resting
with broad shoulders and a bow tightened
i place my pinky on the flat part of the stick
aligning the rest, with it to follow
uncomfortable at first
i try relaxing my hand
loosening the grip
of the violin
to let my chin rest

i am playing notes
accidentally
afraid i'll lose control
over the movement of the bow
i wonder if my skillset
could be categorized as a beginner

although scratchy
they seem to sound good
and the coherence should follow
anytime now
before the string wears out
the bow entangles with my hair
and my eyes lose track
of all the discipline that is to follow
when playing an instrument.

ORIGAMI

You say i blindsided you
but honey, i have corners
even i don't know of
as each day folds a part of me
and creates a new space
i begin learning my design
which is nothing but abstract
and didn't you see the mirrors
which were meant to guide you
or were it the same ones that lost you?

i am sorry
i am undefined

that my edges are not distinct
ragged – like the words i speak

i do not try

to sketch my shape beforehand
afraid of the disappointment
which would follow the end result
after all, i can't bet on how i'll turn out to be
i lie here, flat on the ground
like a helpless object
waiting to be kept in place

now i'm pacing back and forth
hoping you'll create me as a bird
you hang on the top of your loft's ceiling
or maybe you'll create a couple of them
because i had never been enough
to teach you how to

fly,
fly,
fly.

DO YOU NEED A PLACE?

It's okay, i'll close my eyes
if you need a place to cry.

SPIDERS

Mere sight of its gangly legs
penetrates my skin with fear
of being swallowed whole
into an abyss
i stare at the little creature
requiring eight legs for support
to conquer a world
i was too scared to step into
with envy, i watch it crawl confidently
towards a web it has spun
ten times larger its size
evidently, the spider too
had envisioned something big
yet vulnerable, for itself

before it was forced to shed a skin
flipped onto its back
heart rate increasing
slowly pulling itself out
through an opening
and settling into the new skeleton
defenseless –
but with the courage to let itself molt
unlike the rest of us –
terrified of being exposed
to an environment
which only requires for us to
shed our skins

so i kneel on the floor
and let the spider crawl onto my arm
noticing its graceful movement
maybe, it'll let some of its confidence
penetrate through me
mixed with a hint of fear
which is all too familiar.

RESPONSIBILITY

Only you are responsible for
what happens
and doesn't happen
for yourself.

HOW ARE YOU? PART 1

It feels okay now
that "recovery"
i had visualized
for myself

all is not in order

but the thoughts
which were once killing me
seemed to have saved me
from myself

i am not happy

but i am not sad
and that is more than
i had ever envisioned
for myself.

HOW ARE YOU? PART 2

An imminent red nose –
got inspired to fill two canvases with color.

An impending doom –
but yeah, i'm doing good.

IN THE MOMENT

Good or bad, crushes or heartbreaks, solace or
advice – in the moment, we all tend to act irrationally
or even selfish, driven by our emotions. You
shouldn't take it to heart, it's human nature.
However, what I know for sure is that every person
we meet subconsciously takes a place in our minds –
and over time, perhaps when we're alone on a bus or
eating our food – traits and dialogues of these people
creep up on us. Often, we tend to shut our eyes to
avoid the flashbacks, and sometimes we smile. And
one day for both of you, a situation will resonate
with this person and the only question you will ask
is "what happened?" Be sure to be kind, so you don't
hurt yourself in the future by feeling guilty that you
did wrong to someone.

EMPTY WORDS

It isn't your fault –
they say empty words

those
can only
make one feel
like nothing.

HOMESICK

All my life i was told to make family a priority –
so we baked cakes late at nights
stayed up all night with buckets of ice-cream
the carpets still carry stains
from spilled juices
and popcorns
which were squashed under our feet
while dad told us his office stories
backed up with mom's childhood adventures
which we related with
the latest happenings in our schools
as the clock struck past our bedtime
we begged to finish watching the movie
and laughed over the loopholes
we thought existed in the story plot
while pouring our morning cereals
hearing the school bus honk at the door
wishing it'd turn around and leave us be
because even then,
we didn't want to leave the threshold of our homes
but today, stepping outside the door
is more than just a few hours
till we return home
we must leave for
another place
to call our home
instead –
i talk about the family movie nights
with my friends at the lunch table
who are busy counting miles
between their university and home
comparing their distance with mine
to see who'd feel closer to mom
feeling homesick
for a house we had only ever
attempted to sneak out of.

A CONFESSION

I am not
as strong
as i pretend to be.

DESIGNS

Humans are constellations
all over the place –
until, they find their design.

ONE DAY AT A TIME

No matter how detailed you plan
you'll never feel ready
for the big moment

which is meant to transform you –
your life
for good
or for bad

give reasons to wait a bit longer
anticipate for another chance
or a better timing

but it'll always feel rocky
as if the plates under the surface
are re-adjusting themselves
to find a better place

a mountain –

an earthquake –

something significant

best plan one could have:
is to soak it all in
one day at a time.

TATTOOS

Ink stained marks of a harsh memory –

an attempt to make something temporary last

how naïve were we
to say we'd get a tiny rose tattooed
near the edge of our wrists
with each other's initials
in place of a leaf?
insisting that the thorns were left out

hoping it'd be the first thing
anyone noticed upon meeting us
and it'd become an excuse
to mention each other,

a symbol of presence –

and we'd feel ecstatic;
unlike, the prickly needle
which tore the flesh apart
and it hurts more
realizing that this stain
will never wash away.

A PROMISE

I promise i will always
take care of myself.

THE ACT

Sometimes i hold myself back from crying –
as if this act will have the tendency
of proving to myself
that i am strong.

AN OBSERVATION

There is more to life –
than just falling
in and out of love.

DILEMMA

I've been craving a presence beside me
while knowing in my heart
that it is more important
to be self-sufficient

and it feels as if the two
cannot exist together.

YOU ARE MORE THAN YOURSELF

you are more than
who you are aspiring to be –
you are what god intended you to be.

TEA PARTY

Rejecting sturdy bedroom furniture, we settled ourselves on the wobbly plastic chairs, which were often of a bright color – in our shiny, frilly frocks we sat ourselves like sophisticated ladies with our stuffed toys accompanying us faithfully. We said aloud dialogues from teddies in a hushed voice.

The little tea party always tasted sweet despite the presence of water in place of a fancy beverage and that the only form of entertainment came from making up scenarios and taking each other's' comments to heart – and the girls would come in unison if a boy invaded the playroom with their yoyos and paper guns. As this pretense was replaced with clothes of a larger size and real restaurants, more was accounted for than just the number of cups on the table. We carried a bank balance, which would set a limit on the level of frankness on a given occasion.

Although, our acquaintances remained the same, each forgot to carry their own stuff toy which had the capability of mimicking their inner voices – unfortunately, we chose to keep silent; refraining from honest remarks – afraid someone would ask where we bought our high heels from or weather we had visited the newest restaurant around the street where everyone aspired to live. Forgetting, that we had once rejected sophisticated furniture for a fantasy world that had felt more appropriate than reality. Yet, we traded in our tea party for a relatively proper setting, without the promise of ending it on the note that we were all princesses – except from different kingdoms.

AM I BETTER THAN THE REST?

Despite my 5"3 height, I assumed myself to be greater than what I were. I would stride with long steps, pretending as if I had somewhere important to be – when I didn't even know which street led to where. And I'd ask people to wait for me only so I could be fashionably late. Sometimes I'd order food and leave it unfinished on the plate, as if I deserved more than the hard-earned pennies coming out of my parents' pockets – I thought I could have anything, anywhere, and people who complained about life being difficult were only copying the status quo which has become all too mainstream. So, I'd forget the stories my friends would tell me about getting rejected by one university, or not having enough money to buy the dresses displayed in glass windows – I thought they were ridiculing the mere possibility of *getting what you wanted, if you believed hard enough.* And i supposed that is what my mistake was – I had planned my life on a piece of paper, a timeline dictating each event in my life with a pop-up layout of the setting, always accessible in my mind. I'd share with no one; scared they'll copy my ideas or try and get ahead of me. When the only person getting ahead of me was myself. I had a presumption that working in restaurants to pay for your tuition fee was mediocre, that I had to carry a specific phone to be able create a contact list. In my mind, to get everything I wanted only required good timing – which I was always watching out for. My selfish instincts only allowed me to greet teachers for the mere possibility of a shining recommendation and I didn't get too close with people, because cooping myself up in a quiet room; surrounded with charts, sticky notes and daily reminders somehow determined my focus and a path to success - which was nothing but a pile of bricks lining on top of each other, waiting to collapse into a rubble with one wrong move.

So, it came as a shock, when I stood alone with nowhere to go at the moment when I was supposed to be at the places I had dreamt about. I realized I didn't have the power to determine where I stood. Heck, I never had the right to choose the people I surrounded myself with – because I'd be lucky to have anyone standing next to me, when I felt the loneliest and the lost. I had thought I could get anything, that I was better than the rest or that the rest didn't know enough and it was why they were complaining – I had tried to collect flowers to make a garden for myself to rest in, forgetting that flowers are composed of petals and sometimes the petals fall and decay into the ground. But flowers still blossom and although they look the same, some weather harsh winds and others are slowly eaten away by insects, against which they can only fight by staying in one place.

WHICH IS WORSE?

Is there more suffering in
when something is snatched away from us
or if it was never given to us in the first place?

WHY ARE YOU SAD?

I'm afraid –
i am disappointing the people,
who believe(d) in me
and most of all –
i have disappointed myself.

INDECISIVE

In middle school –
i was everywhere
with a soily shirt on the soccer field
behind the red curtains during the school play
singing in the choir,
or sculpting a ceramic block

it wasn't that i were passionate
i'd say they were projects
leading to a sense of accomplishment
why i chose to participate in all
hit me strong when i reached high school

and was given the responsibility
to choose a couple of subjects
a combination –
capable of shaping the rest ahead

i locked myself in the room
with a pencil and paper
trying to connect with my intellectual self
learning that since beginning
i had jumped into every opportunity
led by the fear of regret
my indecisiveness had been my greatest strength

since then –
i never opted for stability
or the lack of risk
or a home base
which pronounces the end
because lost in my own little world
with every option on my fingertips
makes me feel in control
which no subject combination
could have taught me.

WE DON'T WANT PARENTS TO UNDERSTAND US.

As a teenager, I felt my parents exaggerated the fact that they knew me better than myself. I'd lift one eyebrow and leave for the confinement of a room, certain that I was born alone with the unique personality my parents promised I carried – hence, it wasn't possible that anyone could understand me. This helped my prejudiced heart from getting defeated at times by not building high expectations from friends and neighbors, or acknowledging failure by accepting that I was born with a bigger purpose than just facilitating a day-to-day routine. With a belief, so strong, I'd rarely reach out to an older sibling for advice or confide in my mother about the guy who recently broke my heart. With one less person to add a judgment I wouldn't be able to defend; it was easier this way. I believed myself to be stronger than my mother thought I was. Don't get me wrong, I know she supported me and boasted of my potential with whomever in her sights. But how much could a concealer hide? My red puffy eyes would quickly reveal to my mother that I had been crying the night before and she'd force my stubborn self into a hug. With an embrace so strong, who wouldn't let out a tear; and, a heartbeat so loud, I'm sure it echoed in whichever room this unplanned scenario, played out. But that was one day – from a horrible math test, or an argument with my best friend on the phone or that incredibly heartbreaking moment when I'd found out that a boy had lost interest in me. With so much hidden in a cubicle of my heart, I'm afraid those weren't the problems I had claimed were meant to be or not to be understood by my parents. I was afraid of my father finding out that the "f" written boldly in red at the corner of the test report made me doubt my capabilities and in the fruition of hard work, that it wasn't that 5-minute phone call which had ended so abruptly but the loss of trust in friendships which had followed after, and the boy – I swear I didn't even like him as much as I began to fear if any boy would ever want to remain committed to me.

I was never afraid of confiding in the two people who were the reason for my existence, but I was terrified that if I opened to them about the demons in my head, they'll be worried sick for me – and that was worse than them not understanding me. I was never sure of how long those little incidences would make my mood melancholic but I knew that if anyone other than myself knew of what went in my head, they wouldn't just be scared – and it would take a whole lot more strength in the world to repair three broken people than just one.

MY HOUR

Like phases of the moon
your time will come too.

SECOND CHANCES

How often have we begged for them,
only to hear silence or worse;
the question mark at the end of it?

They were life-saving
as a ten-year-old
playing a game of tag.

A risk –
that we'd disappoint ourselves
but isn't this why we pray for them
so we're not held onto by a leash of regret?

I suppose we don't really need second chances
at least not in its physical form
from the very start
we forget to believe in ourselves
that we are more than
more than
we are told to be
or thought to be
we can be or that we are
who we want to be.

Second chances are only a reminder
not to show results to the public's eye
but to open our own perspective
in the way, we view ourselves
and i pray you beg for this second chance
early on in life
than wait for a midlife crisis
so, you know your definite identity
and never hide behind
the curtains
afraid of getting caught.

PIECES

As the skyline splits in two

i remind him:

i had already been a million pieces
before he scattered me across the ocean.

AIRPLANES AND CLOSETS

The sound of airplanes, taking off
balancing at a height i am unable to reach
i do not know if it experiences turbulence
but it's a noise keeping me awake at night
haunting me – that i am stuck in one place

a closet filled with clothes
i were meant to pack
for a place which had promised
me change
has become a pile of unsorted belongings
i cringe at when they touch my body

my fault –
that all along
i had only looked up to the sky
and not crafted wings for myself
which would help my flight
so everything had to transform
with me held in place
and nowhere to move?

LESSON

Nothing is ever
as bad as it seems.

DO YOU STILL WANT HIM?

If i say yes,
i'll lose myself again.

WE HAVE BECOME RESPONSIBLE NOW

Graduating high school became a celebratory event
to bid our friends good-bye
we decorated ourselves with tassels hanging from our caps
took photographs with family –
a proof of how independent
and strong
we had become now
that the scroll in our hands
was enough of a sign
to show we could be trusted
to keep our passports safe
while travelling economy class on our own.

buying a single cup of mocha chino
would soon become a habit
as we walked kilometers at times
just so we can afford a return ticket
on the bus back home,
where we'd cook meals,
packed into boxes
labeled with days of the week –

somehow making us feel better
with the encouragement
that maybe
we have become responsible now.

OPINION

Tuesday 9.00 PM

I was returning home by train today, swiping through my Facebook feed minding my own business. Without invitation, an elderly woman started talking (blabbing) to me and I swear I was only listening to her out of respect. She said the following, and it refuses to leave my mind. Should I think about it or move on?

"I've had a lot to say – wrapped inside a blanket of dogmatism. It protected me from the prejudice I held for the world, which seemed too different for me to fit in. Why do they care? I'd think to myself, make a list of assumptions and cross each one out with a new day to come. I didn't understand the fascination too many of us grew up with – the fascination of getting ahead; but, never with the purpose to outsource a conventional mindset.

I'd get into abrupt fights – the verbal ones – ones that leave a pounding heart and a twitching eye. I've raised eyebrows at teachers, and questioned why in front of relatives; who presumably were my only chance of survival after parents. I've been called over- confident and arrogant and rude.

And I understand it's my fault, that it took me long to understand the difference between reacting and responding. But I'm afraid if I did, I wouldn't be who I am.

I didn't get married at 25; I had kids but not when I wanted to. I've been working my favorite job and have discovered a hobby that instigates passion within me.

I do not own a home, never have I acquired properties. I distributed stickers on election- day, and bunked school the day of the exam. And here I am, exactly the way I had pictured myself 20 years ago, with and without some minor details.

So when I look at the young ones, squabbling over a place in a university or keeping up with the trend of skinny jeans, when they know they'd only be able to breathe in trousers – I tell them, affirmatively – with the hint of opinion I still cannot let go of, I tell them – they'll get to wherever they want to be, but honey, it takes time to make mistakes and you simply cannot skip that part. Because in life, the examiner doesn't carry forward the error and there are no discrete answers.

With dismay, they nod their head sideways, murmuring slang I have not been able to keep up- to- date with and they walk away.

This is why I worry how they will learn in a world that is stealing away the only characteristic that separates them from the rest – an opinion."

HOW TO MANAGE EXPECTATIONS?

Divide your heart into two parts –

tell one of the possibility of everything
setting into place
with just one heartbeat rhyming the others'

like a finely carved sculpture
coming to life
from the piece of paper
which had held its design weeks ago

the other part –
inform it of the scarcity of miracles

so that although,
you'll be on a lookout for them
it'll assure you
there weren't enough
in the world
to begin with.

GARDEN OF YOUR HEART

I am the weed
you pulled out of soil
later to realize,
i too had a life.

MY MAMA USED TO BE A BIRD

I've been advised to walk accompanied on streets lined with hawkers, beggars and wanderers. I should keep my voice low, to avoid unnecessary attention. I should keep my legs closed and my eyes must align themselves with the floor. Mind you, I should not stay up late at night - to steer clear of the dreams I'll manifest in my head before I've gone to bed. I do not ask why, i know the intentions are sincere - that I should be protected and hidden and kept away because I am not an object that anyone can lay their hands on.

But I fly. Ssh, they don't know this.

I have wings and I've seen them unfurl like a carpet unrolls. They're soft - featherlike with a wisp of air which glides through each strand, they smell of lilac and lavender which floats in the air. The scent engulfs itself into a series of circular tornadoes before whispering into my ear. *Fly Fly Fly*. It guides me to lift the delicate feathers above my head.

And I fall.

The weight throws me onto the cold hard floor when I realize I had buried my feet in soil to keep me from falling. I try again, I let go of the control my feet are demanding from the earth. I spread my hands, look up at the sky and guide my body in the direction of the wind.

And I fall.

This time, I move my arms in a forward and backward motion - I fight against the wind which is not being merciful today. As my wings refuse to take flight, I learn that they had always been stronger than myself but they had been considered as an accessory which is now neither of a use to me nor them.

SINCE YOU'VE BEEN AN ADULT

You don't want to be an adult
don't take this to heart,
it is only the nature of time
to engrave labels on a person

you don't want to be here
the place is too dull
and the people don't understand you
but back where you used to live
things have not remained the same

your neighbors –
one won a lottery and moved far away
the other couldn't pay his mortgage
so he did the same

you left snow in your backyard
it has piles of autumn leaves

the bicycle you ride to work now
reminds you of the tricycle
you were gifted by your nana

i know it has been difficult
since you left your parent's home
but trust me –
if you got to travel back in time
you wouldn't want to be
crawling on your knees.

I LOVE YOU

I hope *'i love you'* is the last thing i say to you
when there's nothing else –
left to be heard
so you'll know it's a summary
of all that you mean to me
and not a beginning
hanging onto a string of three words
waiting for a happy ending.

www.ingramcontent.com/pod-product-compliance
Lightning Source LLC
Chambersburg PA
CBHW051435130726
47987CB00005B/2064